BEST BUSINESS GROWTH AND BUSINESS SUCCESS

Growing your Business into a Sustainable Wealth and Income Generator

---

Everything you need to know about business success, wealth management, business intelligence and management of any business; and turning it into a sustainable wealth and income generator!

This is the time to take your business to the next level! Once you have achieved that level and made your business a success, it will be time to take your business to the higher level and maximize profits to double or triple it! Take this as your better business bureau, become a business growth game changer, manage a business efficiently, think big and live large.
Make use of the steps described in this book and utilize business process outsourcing…

And see your business multiply into a sustainable wealth and profit generator.

It's time to start thriving!

Author
Dr Davies M. Mulenga

DEDICATION

I dedicate this book wholeheartedly to you the reader.

Are you an Entrepreneur, a Business Owner or Manager and so on, probably thinking once again the author has dedicated this book to someone else and not you?

Not this time.

This one's for you.

My heart's desire is to help you succeed in your business so that you can help others.

Wishing you all the best of success

Dr Davies M. Mulenga

PhD MScEng EurIng BEng CEng MICE DBA VDI

Before you dive into this book, be sure to claim your Free Bonus: Free Traffic Training on How to Get Tons of Traffic to Your Website Without All the Complicated SEO: http://www.webfire.com/a/?id=29029

In this Free Traffic Training, you will learn how to:

- Instantly get traffic in ANY niche
- Get free exposure from page one of Google, Yahoo, and Bing in 7 minutes or less
- Quickly and easily find people looking to buy what you could be selling
- How to target the traffic that brings in the money instead of fighting over the junk traffic that 99% of everyone else is going for.
- And lots, lots more!

If you would like to partner with us and earn extra income through affiliate commissions signup for free to get started:

http://www.webfire.com/a/?id=29029&aff=1

Bibliografische Information der Deutschen Nationalbibliothek:
Die Deutschen Nationalbibliothek verzeichnet diese Publikation in der Deutschen Nationalbibliografie; detaillierte Bibliografische Daten sind im Internet über http://dnb.dnb.de abrufbar.

©2019 Dr. Davies Mulenga
Herstellung und Verlag:
BoD – Books on Demand, Norderstedt

ISBN: 9783741284168

TABLE OF CONTENTS

STEP 1

KNOW YOUR GOALS

PURPOSE TO CREATE TRAFFIC

DOMINATE SEARCH ENGINES

LEVERAGE YOUR CONTACTS

KNOW YOUR TARGET AUDIENCE

KNOW WHAT MAKES YOU DIFFERENT

OPTIMIZE YOUR ON-SITE CONVERSIONS

EXPAND YOUR LIST

MAXIMIZE YOUR LIST

MAXIMIZE YOUR EXISTING CUSTOMERS

BECOME AN EXPERT

LEVERAGE SOCIAL MEDIA

GO VIRAL

TAP INTO THE POWER OF WEBINARS

CONTINUE TO EXPAND YOUR BRAND

CONTINUE TO EXPAND YOUR SCOPE

CONTINUE TO FOCUS

TO LEARN MORE

A Message from Dr Davies Mulenga

The next several chapters feature some of the greatest tips for completely transforming the state of your business! After you finish reading this book, your business will never be the same again.

As for us, we've been marketing online for a decade, and combined we have hundreds of thousands of customers across the globe.

And to jumpstart your training, we actually created a series of videos for you broken down in how to get more traffic to your sites in any niche easily, how to get free exposure from page one of the search engines in a matter of minutes, how to bypass all the hard work and find people already looking to buy from you, how to stop fighting over all the junk traffic and go straight to the traffic that brings in the dough (that barely anyone is competing for), and lots more! To get this training, go here:

http://www.webfire.com/a/?id=29029

You can also grab this FREE software that sets up money making websites in just a few minutes! No catch. No cost. But you have to get this now because we don't plan to give away the software for long since...

We normally sell this awesome software for $47! Just our gift to you for being our loyal member.

For the Free Software get free access here:
http://www.getfreesoftwarefast.com
To turn your mobile phone into a cash machine visit:
http://crowd1.com/signup/topmillionaire
or
https://www.globalonlineshop.co.uk/
your Sponsor is *topmillionaire*

One more question before we get to the real message of this book: **Looking for New Effective Ways of Expanding your current business?**

Be part of the HOTTEST sector right now with Crowd1 which is exploding globally with over 450,000 new members in just a few short months (as of October 2019). When you see the sector, you will understand the massive affiliate income potential and why 450,000 is just the start. Do NOT Miss this as its hot right NOW! Check out this 37seconds clip

https://www.youtube.com/watch?v=piMtayCVQM0

_____

For detailed information please check

https://www.youtube.com/watch?v=ljUSYRfnfbs

to see why so many people are joining the crowd. It costs nothing to look but this information is time sensitive so I suggest you watch it NOW !

Please get back to the link below as soon as you have watched it. If you have any questions, we will get them answered. If you do not have questions LOCK your spot in Crowd1 NOW and pick a pack today, it takes 1 minute, and YOU will be ahead of the wave. This is going to be HUGE with or without us. Here is your registration link

http://crowd1.com/signup/topmillionaire

For more information also visit

https://www.globalonlincshop.co.uk/

Step 1

Each journey starts with a single step

"Where do I even begin?"

This is the question most people find themselves asking as they aim to expand their business (or as they aim to even get anything going with their business in the first place!). The answer to this often-vexing question? It's actually very simple:

You begin by taking a step!

People tend to get so caught up in the idea of there being a particular "first step" they should take, they end up failing to take any steps at all. What these people fail to realize is that *action* is their greatest ally. They need to take a step. They need to start trying new things. They need to start moving toward the success that is awaiting their efforts!

Of course, it would certainly help to know what a good first step would be, wouldn't it? Well, guess what? You're in luck!

Throughout this book, we are going to be walking you through 100 things you can do to expand your business. We say, in the title, "double or triple" your business, but it doesn't end there! After all, once you have doubled your business…why not double it again? Right? Why not continue to expand your business…and expand it even more…and expand it even more? Why not build an empire?

Not all of these 100 tips are "action steps." Not all of them are specific tasks you can undertake and mark off a checklist. Why? Because every business is unique. Every individual is unique. Each situation is different.

What these 100 items do provide, however, is a sort of roadmap—a sort of guide—to the things that will help you see growth in your business like you've never seen before.

And this is why we are starting at Step 1! Because this is the Step 1 we recommend:

Set aside a weekend.

Seriously. A whole weekend. Heck, we would even go so far as to recommend you rent a cabin in the woods, or rent a suite at a retreat. Get away from your normal life, from your distractions, from your holdups. Change your scenery in order to clear your head. Change your scenery in order to *change your thinking*.

And take this book with you.

Can't afford to spend the money to get away for a weekend? That's fine, too! If that's the case, treat your home like a retreat for the weekend. Leave your phone off. Set aside your responsibilities. Set up a calm, pleasant, quiet atmosphere, and get ready to open your mind, think, and learn.

Listen: this book may be small, but it can change your life. That's not an exaggeration. But guess what? In order for this book to change your life, *you have to do your part*!

This book will present you with a lot of questions—things you should be pondering and answering for yourself. If you read this book front to back in one sitting, it would probably take you an hour or two to get through the whole thing. But if you read this book as you truly should, it will take you the full weekend to reach the end!

Take this book in pieces. Think about every single point. Ask yourself the questions presented and come up with answers. Start sketching out action plans. Start brainstorming new ideas. Start figuring out how you can use the thoughts and tips and ideas in this book to truly take your business to new heights. Start figuring out how you can allow this book to *change your life*.

If you do this—if you truly "retreat" from life for a bit and take this book with you, and truly think through everything (all the thoughts and questions and ideas) presented in this book—you will come out on the other side with a far clearer picture than you have ever had before of what you can do in order to improve your business. Once your weekend of reading and pondering and brainstorming and creative thinking is completed, you will see clearly what you can do to expand your business (and to expand your revenue stream) like never before! Once you finish your weekend of reading, you will know exactly what the *next step* is you should take.

But first thing's first: Step 1. Give this book the time, focus, and dedication it deserves. Give this book a weekend. And get ready to open your mind like never before!

If you want to see a simple but very profitable business idea beforehand, go here: http://www.webfire.com/a/?id=29029&aff=1

If you want to turn your mobile device into a cash making machine install this app and register for free using invite code 465048:

http://invitation.shoppingsherlock.com/465048

Free Software Automatically Creates Money Making Websites here: http://www.getfreesoftwarefast.com

In the next Chapter we will be looking at knowing you goals or setting your goals. Whilst you clearly write down the goals you would like to achieve in your business, please remember to boost the whole process with business success affirmations and gratitude. Gratitude is a powerful process for shifting your energy and bringing more of what you want into your life.

When you use daily goal setting affirmations it keeps your goals right where they should be: in the front of your mind. Planning, focus, perseverance, foresight, dedication, visualization, and hard work will definitely make you achieve any worthwhile goals.

However, practicing affirmations and gratitude will rapidly accelerate your business growth and skyrocket your profits to high figure income based on your set goals. Good sources of information on the subject of affirmations and gratitude are readily available on the internet.

Know Your Goals

Where are you now?

"I'm not reaching my goals.

This is something we often hear people say in regards to their business. When we ask them what their goals are, however, they reply with broad, general statements. In order to achieve your goals, you need to know what your goals are! This will give you a firm sense of purpose and direction in your movement, as you will know exactly what you are moving toward.

Of course, the first step to "knowing your goals" is not figuring out where you want to go. Instead, the first thing you need to determine is this: "Where am I now?"

Before you even move onto the next little section (yup—before you even read the section directly below this one!), we want to encourage you to think about where you are now. Write down some thoughts on where you are now in your progress toward business success. Define your current situation, and put this "definition of your current situation" into concrete form by writing it down. Then, save this definition in a place where you can reference it months from now to see the progress you have made. (And at that point, months from now? You guessed it! You should assess "where you are" again, and should once more write it down to give yourself a new point of reference.)

Go on. Take a moment. Think about it. Define where you are!

Where do you want to be?

Once you have defined where you are, it is time for you to define where you want to be. What are your goals in business? Think about this for a second, and even take a moment to sketch some general thoughts on the place you would like to reach with your business (you can capture these thoughts onto paper, or can simply hold them in your head; you don't have to spend too much time on this, however, because the next thing we want to ask you is…)

Are you projecting big enough?

Small thinking! This is something that prevents so many people from reaching the sort of success they are capable of reaching. When people set their goals, they set them far too small. Essentially, they end up *setting their ceiling too low!*

Now, go back and think about your goals again. Are you limiting yourself? If so, it's time to correct that! It's time to think big. No one is looking. No one is judging. It's just you, this book, and your weekend retreat. Take some time—we'll be here waiting for you when you get back. Break out of the chains that are holding you to "conventional thinking." Go ahead and dive into your "wildest dreams."

In your wildest dreams, what would your goals be for your business efforts?

Take some time to think about this. Write down your thoughts. Be specific (the more specific you are in what your goals are, the likelier you will be to achieve these goals!). And remember: *Think big!!! Check this idea here:* http://crowd1.com/signup/topmillionaire

Take as much time as you need for this, then come back and join us for the next thought we have for you.

What are your limitations?

You've done it, right? We're hopeful that you are actually taking time on each section—that you actually just took some time to think big and write down your "wildest dream" goals for your business (being as specific as possible along the way)—as you will maximize the impact this book has on your life, and on your business, if you are actually taking the time you should be taking to consider the thoughts, ideas, and questions in each section!

Now that we've been a bit stern with you on that (as the kids would say here: "LOL"), we want to ask you this: What are your limitations?

For some of us, our main limitation is our fear of failure.

For others of us, our main limitation is lack of confidence.

Some of us have a hard time focusing, and some of us have a hard time remaining persistent on a long-term project.

Each of us has limitations that are unique to our own self, so…what are your limitations? We'll let you read the next section too before taking another break, because the two go hand-in-hand.

How can you get rid of your limitations?

If "getting rid of your limitations" were as simple as jotting down what your limitations are and spending a few minutes coming up with solutions for getting rid of your limitations, no one would have any limitations at all! As we know, however, it's never quite that simple.

With that said: this harkens back to what we talked about in "Step 1"—the main thing you need to do, in order to accomplish what you want to accomplish, is take a step (then another step, then another, then another). And the first step to shedding your limitations is to identify your limitations, and to start coming up with ways you can destroy your limitations.

So go ahead—take a bit of time. Go for a walk and clear your head and think about this. What holds you back? What keeps you from accomplishing all that you want to accomplish? What are your limitations?

And what can you do to shed your limitations?

We all know that getting rid of your limitations is not as easy as just coming up with some solutions and watching your limitations magically disappear…but it's also important to recognize that limitations will not go away without intentional effort to make them go away. So start thinking about it *now*. Define your limitations so you know what the enemy looks like…then start coming up with a strategy to crush your limitations so that they are no longer holding you back!

Write and read your goals

Welcome back! How was your walk? How was your time coming up with ideas to get rid of your limitations? Hopefully it was successful. Hopefully you are feeling strong enough to beat the world.

We're about to move onto some stuff that is a bit more concrete—in regards to your business success and growth—but before we leave this area of more "intangible" thoughts, we want to make one final recommendation:

Write down your goals. Continue adding to the list as new goals come to you (both short-term and long-term goals; both small-picture and big-picture goals). And read through your list of goals *every single day*.

By writing down your goals and reading them, you will be far more likely to accomplish them. It all starts with a step…and that is one of the greatest steps you can take.

For a good example of how people start business, with a small but giant step go here: http://crowd1.com/signup/topmillionaire simply use "topmillionaire" as sponsor to join the Crowd1 Education and Affiliate Program and you will be up making 6 figure income. More examples here: http://www.shop-on-shop.org

Purpose To Create Traffic

Where does your traffic come from now?

People are always telling us they want to increase traffic on their website, but when we ask people how much traffic they currently get, or where most of their traffic comes from, they have no idea.

Do you have any idea where your traffic comes from? What has worked for you so far? What has failed to work? What are your numbers saying? (And what can you learn from what they are saying?)

What are you doing to create traffic?

Oftentimes, when we ask this question, people get a sort of glazed-over look, as if they are thinking, "I'm supposed to be doing something to bring traffic to my site?"

Yes! Of course you are!

So…how about you, friendly reader? What are *you* doing to create traffic?

Not long from now, we'll be looking at some of the specific things you can do to create traffic for your site, but before we get to that point, we want to encourage you to pause and jot down the things you are currently doing to create traffic for your site, and to list some of the ideas you are able to come up with—off the top of your head—to increase traffic on your website.

What are your traffic goals?

You cannot "reach your goals" until you know what your goals are!

That's pretty important, so we're going to type it again:

You cannot "reach your goals" until you know what your goals are!

So…what are your traffic goals?

Better yet: What are your "wildest dream" traffic goals?

Think about it right now. Write it down. Add it to the list of goals you are reading through each day. And then, it's time to start asking yourself the next question…

How can you get there?

You want to increase traffic, right? Don't move onto the next chapter just yet (as we're about to start digging into the specific things you can do to increase traffic), but first, take a minute to start brainstorming and thinking about this yourself. You may be surprised to discover just how much you already know about traffic generation, and just how much you are able to point yourself in the right direction without any help from us!

You've already written down your goals for traffic. So now, it's time to write down your thoughts on what you can do to get there!

You can also grab this FREE software that sets up money making websites in just a few minutes! It comes with a tip of how to get tons of free websites traffic in about 7 minutes.

Get free access here: http://www.getfreesoftwarefast.com

Dominate Search Engines

Learn SEO

One of the greatest sources of free traffic is search engines. Through search engine optimization (SEO), you can get your website to the top of search engine rankings pages, and can start bringing traffic to your site every single day—through no additional effort on your part—from the Google searches people conduct. In order to make search engines work for you, however, you need to learn the basics of SEO.

Study SEO

Of course, learning the basics of SEO is not enough on its own. In addition to learning the basics of SEO, you need to study SEO.

And then, you need to…

Study SEO some more!

Here's the thing about search engine optimization: You are not the only one who has discovered it! For every search term, there is very limited, relevant search engine real estate. Only ten results show up on Page 1 of Google, and only the top three or four are likely to get a lot of clicks. So just because you have learned search engine optimization does not mean you will suddenly be able to pass everyone else and reach the top of Page 1 for an ultra-competitive search term. SEO is not a secret, and this means that you need to take the time to truly learn SEO—to truly study it until you know it better than your competition knows it.

The cool thing? It's this:

Once you do learn SEO, and study it, and study it some more, you will be able to pass your competition!

You will be able to make the right moves to reach the top of Page 1. And once you have done this, the possibilities for traffic, growth, and revenue on your site will be practically endless!

It's worth it. Take the time: learn SEO, study it, study it some more. http://www.getfreesoftwarefast.com

Apply SEO to your site

Once you have studied SEO to a point where you feel you can truly use it to your advantage, it's time to apply all that you have learned to your website. That's not the end of this story, however. After you have applied SEO to your site, you also need to:

Assess, improve, assess, improve (etc.!)

The search engine optimization on your site can never be "perfect." You know why? Because even once you reach the top of Page 1 for all the search terms you are targeting, your competition will be working that much harder in their efforts to try to pass you and claim that top spot for themselves. This means you need to continually assess your SEO, improve your SEO, assess your SEO again, improve your SEO again, and so on! The good news here is this: Nothing is more powerful than great SEO! And once you gain that top spot, your process of "assessing and improving" will put you in position to continue capturing all the benefits that are coming your way as a result.

Google ads

In addition to search engine optimization, you can use Google ads to ensure you are at the top of search engine rankings pages. Of course, while SEO is free, Google ads cost money. As the old saying goes, however: oftentimes, you have to spend money to make money!

Even once you have reached the top of search engine rankings pages through your SEO efforts, it can be beneficial to have paid ads on Google as well. After all: the more avenues you provide for people to visit your site, the better off your site will be.

Facebook ads

While Facebook is not, strictly speaking, a search engine, it functions in very much the same way, as Facebook possesses a wealth of information on the individuals who are using it. As such, Facebook ads can be just as effective as (or, at times, even more effective than) Google ads.

Before you move onto the next chapter, we want to encourage you to spend some time brainstorming a plan for learning SEO, and to brainstorm some thoughts on how you want to approach using search engines to build traffic to your website.

For an example of websites using SEO for good ranking in search engines check: http://www.gigpanda.com or

http://www.webfire.com/a/?id=29029&aff=1

LEVERAGE YOUR CONTACTS

"I'll promote you if you promote me"

Whom do you know who has a large following online? Whom do you know who has lots of Facebook friends or Instagram followers? Whom do you know who has a popular blog or website?

If the answer is "no one," how about this: Whom can you *get to know* who has a large following?

When two people have followings that do not overlap in many places, it can benefit each party immensely to promote the other. Start thinking through whom you know in order to approach them with this offer: "I'll promote you if you promote me." Even if you do not yet have a large following yourself, you may be surprised to discover just how willing others often are to help you promote your business.

Want to write a guest post?

Even if your website currently receives very little traffic, people are almost always open to the opportunity to write a guest post for another website. By dedicating an area of your site to guest posts (or by making "guest posts" a regular feature on your blog), you will be able to offer people the opportunity to be featured/promoted on your site by providing a guest post. While this seems like a winning proposition for the person writing the guest post (and as you'll see in a moment, it absolutely is), it's also a winning proposition for you, as the person who wrote the guest post is likely to share it with others, and this will lead to extra links for your site (once you learn about SEO, you'll understand just how valuable links are!), as well as extra traffic for your site (and, of course, you already know how valuable traffic is!).

Want to host a guest post?

In addition to making a list of people you want to try to capture a guest post from, you should also come up with a list of popular websites to which you can offer to provide a guest post. When you have a guest post on a site, you will gain exposure to all the readers this site has—which, more often than not, will be an entirely separate audience from the audience you have on your own site. This will mean a lot of opportunity for expansion of site traffic—which, of course, means a lot of opportunity for additional conversions and revenue!

Guest posts for all!

And finally, on top of actively seeking out guest posts for your site, you can make it known on your site that you are open to receiving guest posts. In this way, you will start receiving submissions from readers without having to do any work on your end to gain new guest posts! This will lead to extra content on your site (also important for SEO), extra links, and extra exposure—all with minimal effort from you!

Such contacts could be found here: http://www.shop-on-shop.org
Or by joining the Sherlock Nation Affiliate Program which connects you to thousands of other affiliates and their forums where you can learn how to get exposure and website traffic for free. Become an affiliate here: http://www.shoppingsherlock.com/465048

Know Your Target Audience

<u>Who are they?</u>

One of the greatest things you can do, in order to reach your target audience, is *get to know your target audience.*

This sounds obvious, right? But sadly, this is something most people never do. And honestly, even those who do this often do it wrong!

When we say you should *know your target audience*, we mean you should take steps to truly, honestly, and fully *know them*. We like to go as far as jotting down an idea of exactly what our primary audience looks like! What age range are they in? How are they likely to dress? What do they spend their spare time doing? What would they tell you are their goals, or their desires?

The more fully you know your target audience, the more equipped you will be to reach them. It may seem like a silly thing to do, but seriously—trust us. Take a moment away from this book and write down some words to sketch what your target audience looks like. You don't have to come up with a full, detailed list of your entire target audience right now (although it certainly wouldn't hurt if you did!), but you should at least get a general sketch down on paper. And if you don't get into details right now, make a note to come back to that later in your "weekend retreat" for reading this book and learning how to build your business. The more detailed your idea of what your target audience looks like, the more equipped you will be to truly reach your target audience in the most effective manner possible.

As you sketch your "target audience," be sure to include your answers to the following questions about them.

What websites do they spend time on?

Once you understand the websites on which your target audience is spending its time, you will be able to take this one step further and ask: What is it about these websites that appeals to my target audience?

After that? You guessed it! You can ask yourself, "How can I turn my website into a site they like to spend time on as well?"

Where do they spend money?

You want your target audience to spend money on your site, don't you? Okay, so how about starting out by determining where they currently spend their money! By determining where your target audience is likeliest to spend their money, you can figure out how you will be able to appeal to them on your site, and will be able to encourage them to part with their money on your site as well!

What appeals to them?

In all of this, what you are trying to figure out is: What appeals to them?

In addition to the specific areas listed above, you need to figure out what appeals to them in a fundamental sense—in life, in general. Remember: the more detailed your sketch (or sketches) of your target audience (and of course: your target audience can have lots of different types of people in it, and each "different type of person" should truly have their own sketch, in order for you to best determine how to reach each person you are attempting to reach), the more equipped you will be to reach them.

What speaks to them?

The best way to address an individual is not at the place where they are, or in the way they see their own self. Instead, you want to address an individual—a prospective customer or client—at the place where they *want to see their own self*.

We're going to type that again to make sure you fully grasp that idea. Don't skip over it! It's a short paragraph; read it again!

The best way to address an individual is not at the place where they are, or in the way they see their own self. Instead, you want to address an individual—a prospective customer or client—at the place where they *want to see their own self.*

What "speaks to" most people is not communication that meets them where they are. Instead, what "speaks to" most people is communication that addresses them in the place where they want to be—or that addresses the person they want to grow into or become. By determining how your potential customers or clients *want to see themselves*, you will be able to speak to *those* individuals, rather than speaking to the individuals they are in the present. This will have a massive impact on the ability you have to get your message through!

How can you best target your target audience?

Remember: be as detailed as you can possibly be in your sketch of your target audience. Figure out who they are, and figure out who they want to be, and it will then be easy for you to jot down ideas of how you can best target this target audience.

So, what are you waiting for? It's time to "hit the drawing board"! It's time to take a break from this book and sketch your target audience. It's time to figure out who they are, who they want to be, and how you can create a message that will have the greatest possible impact as a result!

You could make a simple comparison between this website http://www.globalonlineshop.co.uk/ for products with a marketplace website: http://www.shop-for-shop.co.uk to see which website will get great results looking at a specific target audience.

Know What Makes You Different

Who are your biggest competitors?

You would not fight a war if you did not know who your enemy was.

You would not try to play a sports event without knowing which team you were supposed to be playing.

So why do so many people try to "win at business" without even knowing who they are trying to beat? Listen: every client or customer you gain is a client or customer you have to win. More than likely, you are not the only person, company, or business offering the general product or service you offer, which means that—in addition to convincing people they need to purchase your product or service—you need to keep them from purchasing this product or service from someone else; you need to ensure they are purchasing it from *you*.

So—how about it? Get that notebook out! Take some time to think about it, and write down a list of who your biggest competitors are.

Who are your fiercest competitors?

Not only do you need to worry about your "biggest competitors"—the competitors whose names everyone already knows—but you also have to worry about your "fiercest competitors." These are the competitors who are in the same place as you (or who are maybe even lower than you) in the business ladder in your particular area of focus. Over time, it will be your "fiercest competitors" who will be likeliest to cause you problems. By identifying your fiercest competition *now*, you can figure out the ways in which you can become their fiercest competition in return. You may win some against this "fierce competition" over time, and you may lose some over time, but by identifying them now, you will be in much better shape to "win" more often than not.

What makes their websites stand out?

Do some reconnaissance! Visit the websites of all your competition. Like a General studying troop movement or a coach watching game film of an opponent, you should be spending time on your competitors' websites to get to know them as best you can.

Once you have your list of who your "biggest" and "fiercest" competitors are, you can make a list of the things that make each of their websites stand out. Then, add to the list the following items…

What do they do well on their websites?

When you visit each competitor's website, what stands out to you as "things they do well"? Explore their sites to answer this question, then write down the things each of your competitor websites do well.

What do they do poorly on their websites?

In addition to determining what each site does well, you want to know what each site does poorly! Look at their site from the perspective of a prospective customer or client; what are the things on each site that would turn you away?

What do they do well in their business?

As you spend time studying each of these websites—and as you subsequently spend time studying each business as a whole—you should also jot down each thing you notice that they do well in business. Of course, the flip side of this is also in play…

What do they do poorly in their business?

As you study each business, also take note of the things they do poorly! By identifying the things each of your competitors do poorly, you will be effectively identifying "chinks in the armor" that you will be able to exploit.

Where can you incorporate the "good"?

Now that you have made a list of who all your competitors are (you have done this…right?) and have spent time exploring each of their sites, determining what they do well and what they do poorly, and determining what draws your attention while also determining what pushes you away, it's time for you to use this knowledge to improve your own site, your own business, and your own capacity for success!

Of the "good things" these other websites, companies, and businesses do, which can you incorporate into your own approach? And how can you incorporate these things?

Where can you gain an edge in the public eye?

And, of course, now that you have identified the weaknesses your competitors have, you will be able to identify the ways in which you can gain an edge in the public eye!

This is one of the most important chapters in the book, so we hope you are not simply flying through it and moving onto the next one. We hope you are, instead, actually taking the time to determine what your competition looks like, and to assess the ways in which you can gain an edge! Once you have taken the time to do this, you will be astonished at just how much you have realized, and at just how easy it is for you to incorporate the "good things" your competition does, and to gain an edge on your competition by exploiting the things they do wrong!

Again compare the http://www.globalonlineshop.co.uk/ with website of major retailers selling similar products on the internet. This will give you an idea on how to incorporate the "good things" your competition does.

Go here for a better example: http://gr8.com/pr/fE45C/d

Or http://shop-on-shop.org/

Optimize Your On-site Conversions

What is the purpose of your site?

Welcome back!

(Well...at least, we hope this is a "welcome back." We hope you've been away for a bit doing all the things we advised you to do in the last chapter!)

Now that we have spent time focusing on your target audience and focusing on your competition, it's time for us to turn or focus to *you*. To *your business*. To *your site*.

The first thing we have to ask, then—in turning the attention to you—is this:

What is the purpose of your site?

This is not a philosophical question. It's not a trick question. Instead, it's a core question you need to ask yourself. And we're going to help you out by giving you the answer:

The purpose of your website is to convert visitors into customers!

No matter what product you sell, no matter what service you offer, no matter who your target audience is or who your competition is, the fundamental purpose of your website will always be the same: to convert visitors into customers.

Write that down.

Remind yourself of that every single day.

Let everything you do on your website be directed by that knowledge.

The purpose of your website is to convert visitors into customers! For more tools visit this website http://shop-on-shop.org/

Does each new article on your site lead to conversions?

Now that you know this—now that you understand that the only thing that truly matters on your site, in the long run, is whether or not you are converting visitors—you can start making sure that your focus, in everything you do on your site, is pointed in this direction.

That means that each new article or piece of content you write on your site should be written with this idea in mind:

The purpose of your website is to convert visitors into customers!

Each new article or piece of content you write on your site should be written with the purpose of, ultimately, converting visitors.

Does each old article on your site lead to conversions?

On top of making sure that the focus of each new article or piece of content you create is appropriately directed, you need to start going back through old articles or pieces of content on your site! Did you write these with the mere purpose of using keywords? Did you write these with the mere purpose of providing information?

Look: Keywords are important. Providing information is important. But in every piece of content, you also need to have little things that are intentionally in place in an effort to nudge the reader toward a conversion.

Take a moment and come up with an action plan of how you can gradually adjust your old content so that it is all geared toward conversions. By taking this project bit by bit, you will eventually be able to overhaul all your old content, and will be able to drastically increase the impact this old content has on your bottom line.

Does every single page on your site lead to conversions?

In addition to overhauling old content, you also need to look at every static page on your site. Examine each page from the perspective of a prospective customer visiting the site for the first time. Imagine that each particular page is the first page they landed on. What does the page do to capture their attention right away—to stand out from the competition? And then, what does each page do to nudge the visitor toward a conversion?

What is working, and what is not?

As you focus in this area, you also need to make sure you are continually assessing and examining what is working and what is not. Which pages on your site are leading to more conversions? Which pages on your site are keeping visitors around longer? Which pages on your site are failing to lead to conversions, or are failing to keep visitors around on your site? Continually assess, and continually improve! In this way, you will ensure that your website continues to grow stronger and stronger, and that you continue to put more space between you and your competition.

See example of optimized website here: http://gr8.com/pr/fE45C/s or http://shop-on-shop.org/

Expand Your List

If you haven't already, set up an email list

If you have been doing Internet marketing for any length of time, you know that one of the most important things for success is a quality email list.

This is pretty common knowledge with regards to Internet marketing, right? And yet, most people who have been dabbling in Internet marketing for a year or two or even three do not have an email list at all!

We file this under the issue discussed earlier in this book: people sometimes are so overwhelmed in trying to decide what their "first step" should be, they end up taking no steps at all!

You know what your first step should be in this area? Your first step should be to set up an email list! You cannot progress in this area until you first set up a list—so step up to the plate and set up a list! See signup example here: http://www.getfreesoftwarefast.com

Set up a place on each page for people to sign up

After you have set up an email list, you need to make sure there is a place on every single page on your site where people can sign up for your email list. Make sure that it is prominently visible and pointed to in order to capture as many email addresses as you can possibly capture!

Set up a place on each article for people to sign up

The same thing goes for every single article on your site. Remember in the last chapter, when we talked about how the entire goal of your site is conversions? Well, this is one of the best ways to create conversions—and this means that you should be focusing on pointing people toward the opt-in for your email list at every single opportunity you have to do so—including every single page on your site, and every single article you post!

Create an incentive for people to sign up

But here's the thing: every website people visit these days will be trying to get them to sign up for their email list—right? So in order to get people to sign up for *your* email list, you need to stand out from the crowd! What can you provide people for signing up that they cannot receive elsewhere? By giving people a truly valuable incentive for signing up for your email list, you will get far more conversions than you have ever experienced before.

Tie your list into your content—constantly!

And, of course, you need to make sure that your email list never feels like an "afterthought" to those who are visiting your site. In every piece of content on your site, you should aim to mention your newsletter or your mailing list at least once—in a casual, natural manner. By continually tying your mailing list into your content, you will keep it in the minds of your readers. They may not opt in the first time they come to your site; they may not opt in the second time or the third time or even the tenth time! But if you continue to promote your list and tie your list into your content and encourage visitors to sign up, you will continue to grow your list and grow your list and grow your list!

Before moving onto the next chapter (where we will be talking about the things you can do to maximize your list), we want to encourage you to take some time away from this book and come up with a plan of how you can increase opt-ins on your site. Where can you feature the opt-in opportunity on each page and article? What incentive can you provide? And how can you start tying your list into your content constantly? By coming up with a plan, you will be in better position to execute your plan, and will be able to move closer to the goals you have in this area!

See good example here: http://www.getfreesoftwarefast.com

Or http://shop-on-shop.org/

Maximize Your List

What value can you provide from your list?

Hopefully you are returning from a break, and have just finished coming up with ways in which you can increase your list! Now that you have done that—now that you are on track to start increasing the number of opt-ins you have—it is time to start thinking about the ways in which you can maximize your list, in order to use it to truly boost your business.

The first way in which you can start maximizing your list is by providing actual, genuine value. You know why most people don't like signing up for email lists? Because most email lists are nothing but an obvious ploy for the person running the list to promote products and make money! Sure, you want to do the same thing (you want to promote your products or services; you want to make money), but that cannot be the reason for people to sign up for the list. Instead, people need a reason that is beneficial for them to sign up for the list! In other words: people need you to add value to their life.

How can you provide value on your list? How can you use a monthly newsletter (or a similar, regularly-scheduled interaction with your list) to provide benefits for your readers? How can you add value to the life of each of your readers…so that each of your readers can add value to you?

What consistent theme will keep people excited about reading?

Because we assume you are not pausing each time we suggest you pause from this book—because you are probably continuing to read most of the time—we assume you did not pause after reading that last section, and instead chose to keep reading. Are we right? Well, if we are, that's totally fine, as this section will help you come up with a plan for how you can add value! In fact, if you'd like, you can feel free to read this entire chapter before pausing to plan out how you can start maximizing your list.

In order to provide value to your readers, one thing you need to realize is that you need to give your readers something they look forward to reading! And one of the best ways to make sure your readers are going to look forward to reading what you have for them is by making sure you keep a consistent theme in each newsletter you send out. When readers know what the general theme will be, they will be far likelier to stick around, and will be likelier to engage each time they receive an email from you.

What will get your readers to share with others?

Another great way to build your list is for your readers to share your list with others. This can be through talking about your list in person or online, or through sharing links online with their friends, business contacts, clients, etc. As such, one question you need to be asking yourself is this: What will get people excited about sharing my list with others? What am I telling them, showing them, revealing to them, or explaining to them that will be so important—that will have so much of an impact—they cannot help but share with others?

In every single newsletter or email blast you send out, you should be focusing on providing valuable knowledge and content that your readers will be excited to share with others—that your readers, in fact, will not be able to help but share with others!

Are you profiting off your list?

You do not need to profit off your list in an absolutely direct manner (as in: you do not need to sell products through the emails you are sending out—although you certainly can do this!), but you do need to make sure that you are intending to create profit through your list. This can be through directing people to certain products or upsells of yours; it can be through making sure each email you send out will lead to your readers bringing more readers your way; it can be through leading people to a page on your site that is intended to convert them to a new purchase; or, it can simply be through engaging with them in such a way that they remain committed to your brand! But regardless of the form this takes, this is something you need to make sure you are focusing on. You need to make sure you are using your list to profit!

Keep current clients engaged

We've mentioned "engagement" several times. To clarify what we mean by this: the reader should feel like you are talking to them! The reader should feel like they have a relationship with you. The reader should be encouraged to ask questions and think about things and interact with the emails they are receiving from you. In this way, they will remain engaged…and in this way, they will continue to look forward to your newsletter each month, and will continue to provide value to you, through your email list.

Push clients to be involved off-site

In each newsletter or email blast you send out, one of your goals should be to encourage your readers to promote your site, your business, your product, or your newsletter off-site. Now, you need to realize that it is rarely effective to come right out and ask readers to "share with others," or to request that readers help you spread the word. In fact, this often sounds like desperation to readers! Instead, you need to make sure you are providing tremendous value…and then you need to subtly—and regularly—drop hints that will encourage people to share your site, product, business, etc., with others.

Free giveaways

Using your list to give away products is another great way to maximize your list! If you regularly give away information products through your list (perhaps products you have created specifically for the purpose of giving away), you will provide plenty of value that cannot be provided in any other way.

Upsell new products of yours

And, of course, one of the best ways to make sure you are actually turning profit from your list is by upselling products to your readers! This does not need to be done in a blatant or "salesy" manner; instead, you can "feature" different products of yours each time you send out an email to your list, and you can also tie in thoughts about products you have for sale throughout the content you provide. By casually mentioning products at every chance you have to do so, you will continually remind readers that they can purchase products of yours, and this will lead to a continual increase in sales.

Upsell information products of others'

Finally, realize that you do not only have to sell your own products through your list. You can also sell information products that others have! As you become an affiliate for different information products, you will be able to promote these products to your list, and will be able to receive a commission for each and every product that is sold. This is one of the best ways to maximize the profit you are squeezing out of your list!

Now, this chapter is over…and you know what that means, don't you? We don't know if you will listen to us, but we sure hope you will: we want to encourage you to take a bit of time and come up with a plan on how you can maximize your list, following the guidelines listed in this chapter!

After you have taken the time to do that, we'll see you in the next chapter—where we'll be talking about maximizing your existing customers!

To learn more about upsells and how to get buyers in the upsell funnel go here and look for Education Packages:

http://crowd1.com/signup/topmillionaire

Maximize Your Existing Customers

What does your ideal customer look like?

If you have paid attention to the world of business, you know that the majority of your business will come from a small percentage of your clients. You also know that it costs a lot more to gain a new client than to keep an existing client. As such, one of your core focuses—as you aim to increase business and increase revenue—should be focusing on the customers you already have!

Remember earlier in this book when you sketched out your target audience? Well, we want to encourage you to do something similar here…but this time, we want you to sketch your ideal customer!

As you did before: take a break. Think this through. Come up with a clear picture of what your "ideal customer" looks like. What are their interests? Where do they spend money? What sort of work do they do for a living? What do they spend money on?

Once you have a clear, firm idea of exactly who your "ideal customer" is, you will be able to then move onto the next question, which is:

How can you better appeal to your ideal customer?

Once again, we want to encourage you to truly take a moment and figure out what your ideal customer looks like. Pause from reading. Go for a walk. Sort through your thoughts. Sketch out your ideal customer. Maybe you don't even have any customers at the moment; that's okay! Maybe you are just getting started in the world of Internet marketing or entrepreneurship or business, and you don't have any idea yet who your "ideal customer" is, as you are just hoping—at the moment—to get any customers at all. That's perfectly fine. Even if this is the case, we want to encourage you to sketch out your ideal customer, because your business is going to keep expanding! Your business is going to grow. And once it does, you will have ideal customers, and you will need to be able to spot them.

After you have sketched what your "ideal customer" looks like, then, it will be time for you to take the next step: you need out what you will be able to do to appeal to your ideal customer. You already know what they look like, right? You know their desires, their interests, and their general take on life. So now, it's just one more small step forward to figure out what you can do to appeal to them!

How can you improve their experience?

In addition to figuring out how you can appeal to your ideal customer, we want to encourage you to put yourself in their shoes. Ask yourself what the experience of purchasing products or services from your site is like for them…and then, ask what you can do to improve their experience.

How can you make them feel important/special/rewarded?

One of the best ways to improve a customer's experience is by making sure they feel important, special, and rewarded. So, again: put yourself in their shoes. What is likely to make them feel important/special/rewarded? And how can you continually take steps to ensure that this is exactly how your "ideal customers" feel?

How can you make sure they are loyal to you for life?

It cannot be said enough: it costs more to obtain a new customer than to keep a current customer! As such, you should constantly be focusing on what you can do to keep your current customers.

What will cause customers to feel loyal to you? What will cause them to feel connected to you?

Remember: you know exactly what your target audience looks like. You know exactly what your ideal customer looks like. This makes it an easy step for you to then figure out what will make these people feel committed to your brand. After all: you already know them, right? So it's only one extra step to figure out what will appeal to them, and what will keep them around for life.

Before moving onto the next chapter, we would certainly not discourage you from reading this chapter again, as we feel there is a lot of important information in this chapter you should be pondering—information that will help you truly maximize your clients like never before.

Once you've done that (and have taken the time to map out anything you need to map out after having read this chapter), it is time to turn the focus more fully onto you, as we will begin looking at the importance of becoming an expert—and of how you can become an expert yourself and turn this "expertise" into profits!

Again check this examples:

https://www.globalonlineshop.co.uk/

Is this the New Lazy Man's Way to MAKE MONEY? Get Free Book here: http://shop-on-shop.org/

Become An Expert

Who are the "experts" in your area?

One of the most important things you can do, in order to maximize the impact your efforts have, is to reach a point where you are viewed as an "expert" in your area of focus. When you are viewed as an "expert," it will become exponentially easier for you to make sales, for you to keep the customers you have, and for you to rapidly expand to gain new customers.

"But…I'm not an expert."

If this is what you are thinking, that's totally fine. Because here's what's great about being an "expert": anyone can become one! It's all about knowing how to approach the issue of being viewed as an expert:

https://dr-davies-school.thinkific.com/courses/how-to-become-an-expert-in-your-niche

The first step to becoming an expert? You need to determine who are the experts in your area of focus. Who do people look to for their definitive information? Who to people look to for learning and knowledge? Who are the experts in your area?

You may know the answer to this question already, but if you don't, go ahead and take a bit of time to figure out exactly who the "experts" are in your area of focus.

What do they offer?

No one is an expert just for the sake of being an expert; instead, every expert has built to this place of being viewed as an expert in order to offer things to those who listen to them. Sometimes, they offer advice; sometimes, they offer information; sometimes, they offer tips; sometimes, they offer benefits that are more intangible. Before you can start moving toward becoming an "expert" yourself, you need to identify who the experts in your area of focus are, and then you need to figure out what these experts are offering. Why? Because the next step is asking this:

How can you incorporate what they offer?

Once you have identified what these "experts" offer, you will be able to start finding ways to incorporate these same things yourself. After all, these "experts" are viewed as experts for a reason—and that reason, more often than not, is the simple fact that they have a large audience! If they have a large audience, they are obviously doing something right in order to appeal to and keep this audience…and once you start incorporating those same things yourself, you will be able to start seeing similar results.

Is this the New Lazy Man's Way to MAKE MONEY? Get Free Book here: https://dr-davies-school.thinkific.com/courses/how-to-become-an-expert-in-your-niche

How can you offer something different?

Of course, it's not all about offering the same things that other experts offer! You also need to take this one step further and ask: what can I offer that will set me apart?

What is "being an expert" all about?

All of this may seem a bit confusing, of course, if you do not quite have a firm grasp of what being viewed as an "expert" actually entails, but the good news is this:

"Being an expert" is actually quite simple! In fact, the idea behind "being an expert" can be broken down into three core ideas.

1. Platform

An expert has a platform from which they can share their thoughts. Usually—ultimately—this is their own website, but that is not ever the full extent of "being an expert," and is rarely where these experts got their start.

Most experts also have social media platforms (more on that in the next chapter), and most experts also have other sites they write for! If you're now thinking, "Well, great for them, but I don't have other sites I can write for," the cool thing is this: you're absolutely wrong! Sites are always looking for content. And as soon as you have been published on a well-known site, your credibility as an "expert" will skyrocket!

Start looking for opportunities to write for other sites. You may need to start with smaller sites, but this will get your foot in the door with bigger sites…which will get your foot in the door with bigger sites…and so on! Before long, sites will be asking you to write for them, and readers will think of you as an expert!

2. Knowledge

Of course, "platform" is not everything, as you also have to have knowledge. This should go without saying…but sadly, it doesn't, as people seem to always be trying to boost their "expert status" without actually having any knowledge!

While it may seem, however, as though you would have to have a vast amount of knowledge in order to be viewed as an "expert," this is not the case either. Instead, you simply need some knowledge that others don't have. By taking just a bit of time to study your area of focus, you can quickly gain knowledge that others don't have; by disseminating this knowledge on well-respected platforms, your status as an "expert" will be solidified quickly!

https://dr-davies-school.thinkific.com/courses/

3. Image

And finally, one of the most important aspects of being an "expert" is the image you project. You see, people do not want to listen to advice from someone who keeps telling them they are "learning as they go," or who keeps saying they are "hoping to become an expert." Even before you see yourself as an expert, you need to project yourself as an expert to readers! If you can make readers see you as an expert, the battle is already won.

Turn your status as an expert into profits

All that remains, once you are viewed as an expert, is for you to turn your status as an expert into profits. Information products are the best way to do this, as people always want to learn what an expert has to say! But even if you do not want to write your own information products, you can leverage your status as an "expert" to sell information products that others have written, and to make money as a result.

The main thing to realize about being an "expert," however, is that—ultimately—people want to listen to and pay attention to the things an expert has to say! So as soon as you are able to put yourself in position where you are viewed as an expert, you will see a lot more traffic coming to your site, and you will be able to focus on converting this traffic in order to get the most out of this ultra-positive development!

So, how about it? How can you start turning yourself into an expert, and how can you start profiting as a result?

Don't tell us! We aren't the ones who need to know. Take some time, think about it, and come up with a plan for yourself.

Becoming an expert is one of the most valuable things you will ever do in your business efforts, so take your time on this. Ponder this. Come up with a quality plan in order to be able to turn yourself into an expert!

Some experts you can work with are here:

http://www.webfire.com/a/?id=29029&aff=1

Is this the New Lazy Man's Way to MAKE MONEY? Get Free Book here: https://dr-davies-school.thinkific.com/courses/how-to-become-an-expert-in-your-niche

Leverage Social Media

<u>Use Twitter to disseminate information, connect, and provide value</u>

Social media is everywhere these days, and if you are not on social media yourself, you are not going to be able to get as much out of your online efforts as you would ultimately like to be getting. In this chapter, we are going to be looking at the best ways in which you can focus your social media efforts in order to improve your business—and the first way in which you can use social media to your advantage is by using Twitter to disseminate information, connect with others, and provide value.

If you do not have a Twitter account, you need to set one up. At first, it may seem as though you are talking to yourself on there…but as you continue to work to build your platform as an "expert," you will continue to increase your following on Twitter, and will consequently increase the impact Twitter has for you.

Because Twitter has developed into a platform that is primarily used for people to absorb information and knowledge from individuals they trust and/or respect, it has become one of the best ways for businesses and entrepreneurs to stay connected with customers, and to bring new customers into the fold. You should aim to spend a good 30 to 45 minutes on Twitter each day, sharing information and thoughts, and doing the next item on this list as well:

Use Twitter to interact!

Another element of Twitter that has made it what it has become is the fact that people can use Twitter to interact with the experts they love gaining information from. You know what this means for you, right? You are setting yourself up as an expert…and this means you need to also be taking the time to interact with those who are on Twitter, in order to become one of those "experts they are getting to interact with"!

Use Instagram to connect, interact, and pull to your site

Instagram is quickly becoming the most powerful social media platform, and this means that you need to be on there!

This will take a bit of creativity on your part, as you will need to figure out exactly how you can use pictures to tie into your message. But the great thing about Instagram is that it has a community that is extremely interactive and conversational. By coming up with a plan for how you can use Instagram to connect, interact, and pull people to your site, you will be able to tap into the power of this community yourself.

https://dr-davies-school.thinkific.com/courses/

Use LinkedIn to connect with customers

Of course, for business, nothing beats LinkedIn for connecting in ways that will benefit your scope of influence. One of the best ways you can use LinkedIn is by connecting with customers you already have! Because your current customers are your most valuable asset, connecting with them directly and personally on a social media platform (asking about their experience working with you, asking for advice on ways you can improve, etc.) can go a long way toward keeping them loyal to you for life!

Use LinkedIn to create opportunities

You can also use LinkedIn to connect with other business owners and influencers in your area of expertise. The more connections you have, and the more involved you are in the business community in your particular area of focus, the more of an impact you will ultimately be able to have. LinkedIn, then, becomes a great way to connect with others who can help you expand your own brand.

Use Facebook to build brand loyalty

Of course, Facebook is another one of the best ways to build brand loyalty, as Facebook is a very personal platform—a place where people usually go to connect with and keep up with close friends and family members. By making your Facebook page a regular destination for customers, you can build massive amounts of brand loyalty, as they will associate your products, services, or brand with their personal life!

Use Facebook to expand

Facebook is also a great way to expand your business. We already talked about Facebook ads earlier in the book, but in addition to Facebook ads, you can use Facebook to run giveaways and promotions that will help to get your brand, your name, and your product in front of people who might not otherwise have seen them! Again, remember: Facebook is interactive, personal, and—when it comes down to it—far more intimate than any other social media platform. As such, your ability to connect with current customers on Facebook will go a long way toward increasing your ability to make money in your business in general!

Use Facebook to drive sales

In everything you do on Facebook, you should be focused on "driving sales"—while never making it apparent to Facebook visitors that this is your focus! In other words: people are not on Facebook to be "sold" tings, so you do not want to be overly aggressive in your efforts to use Facebook in this manner. And yet, "sales" are ultimately your main focus, as this is what drives your profits. As such, you want to use

Facebook to subtly drive sales—and this should be the core focus behind every single thing you do on that site.

Expand your social media thinking

Of course, in addition to the core social media platforms mentioned above, you should also aim to expand your social media thinking. There are tons of social media platforms, with new ones being added seemingly every day! Start finding some of the other social media platforms on which your message can find a home, and make an effort to use these platforms to expand your brand. You may be surprised just how much of a difference it can make to be in on the ground floor of a smaller social media platform.

Encourage sharing from your site

Finally, realize that everything on your website should be tied into social media. After all, most people's lives are tied into social media—right? So shouldn't your website be tied into this area where most people's lives are tied?

By encouraging social media sharing from your site, you will constantly receive a trickle of sharing you would not otherwise have received…which will lead to a trickle of traffic you would not otherwise have received…which will continue to grow, and grow, and help your business expand!

What can you be doing on social media for your own business? What are you doing currently, and what is your plan to expand? https://dr-davies-school.thinkific.com/courses/

Go Viral

Create a valuable video

We know, we know—everyone wants their videos to "go viral," right? So what makes us think you can be one of the few who can create a viral video yourself?

Good question. Luckily, we have a good answer as well:

Because you've now set yourself up as an expert! Expert's videos get shared. Sure, it may not "go viral" in the "Charlie bit my finger" sense…but your videos will get shared without you doing any work on your own, and this is a tremendous benefit for the bottom line of your business.

In order to make this happen, however, you first have to do your part—and one of the ways in which you can do this is by *creating valuable videos*. When you create valuable videos—with valuable information, as an "expert"—these videos will be viewed, and they will be shared, and they will benefit your business.

Create a video series

In addition to creating valuable videos, a great way to truly take advantage of the power of videos is by creating video series. This, of course, takes the same idea we have behind "creating valuable videos," and it expands it to include a number of videos that will keep people engage, as they will be looking forward to the next installment in the video series. If you are able to take an idea and turn it into a series of videos, this can have a massive impact on your business—especially once you have already set yourself up as an "expert."

Many people get trapped in thinking that they don't have anything to share in a single video—let alone in a series of videos. But we want to encourage you to take some time and map out some video ideas. Guess what? You just may end up being surprised to find what you come up with! Try to come up with ten video ideas—ten things you can share from your position as an "expert," and after you have finished reading this book, come up with a plan and a timeline for how and when you will make these videos.

Stay in your comfort zone!

If you are not a high-energy person, don't think that you have to be one simply because you are creating a video. The more comfortable you are in your video, the more comfortable your viewers will be—and, of course, the more comfortable your viewers are, the more of an impact your videos will have.

We'll tell you right now: your videos are probably not going to be a smash hit from the get-go! But as you take the "first step" of making them, and as you then make an effort to assess and improve and assess and improve (etc.!), you will continue to turn your videos into something truly worth watching…and this will truly help your business a ton.

Ask: What do people want?

As you continue to assess and aim to improve, one question you need to keep asking yourself is: What do people want? Pay attention to comments and feedback to see what people like and dislike in your videos, and make sure you are constantly striving to provide your viewers with what they want.

Ask: How can I provide it?

Realize that knowing what your viewers want is not the same as providing viewers with what they want! In addition to knowing what your viewers want, you need to also make sure you are always asking yourself how you can provide viewers with what they want; this will enable you to continually engage with your audience in exactly the right place for them, and to continually get the most out of your video content. http://www.globalonlineshop.co.uk

See some wants here: http://www.shop-on-shop.org/

Tap Into The Power Of Webinars

Use your webinar to share valuable information

The webinar is one of the greatest ways to leverage your platform as an "expert," as it provides you with an opportunity to use video in an interactive and instructive manner, while also enabling you to convert a large number of sales. Honestly, if you are not exploring webinars, you are cutting yourself short of the profits you have the capacity to make—especially once you have established your expert platform.

Once you begin exploring webinars, the first thing you will need to make sure you are doing—in order to get the most out of your webinars—is *sharing valuable information*. Anyone can put together a webinar that is filled with filler, but not everyone has the ability to share truly valuable information in their webinar. If you are able to become one of the "experts" whose webinars are known for being full of truly valuable information, you will have an easy time creating massive amounts of brand loyalty through your webinars, and will be able to expand your brand rapidly as well.

Use your webinar to create brand loyalty

This is, in all honestly, a byproduct of a solid webinar. If you are presenting truly quality, valuable information in your webinar, you will create brand loyalty along the way. It is important, however, for you to realize that this is the case, as "realizing that this is the case" will enable you to purpose toward "brand loyalty creation" within your webinar. The more you search for little ways to increase brand loyalty throughout your webinar, the more you will enhance the brand loyalty that would naturally occur.

Use your webinar to boost your list

This is *not* something that will occur naturally through a webinar, but it is something with which you can have a massive impact if you focus on it intentionally. Your webinar is one of the best ways to grow your list—so as you run your webinar, be intentional about promoting your list, as this will help you create great results in this area.

https://dr-davies-school.thinkific.com/courses/

Use your webinar to boost sales

And, of course, the entire point of the webinar—on your end—is to increase sales. Now, it should not be visible or obvious to the viewer of the webinar that this is the core focus, but it is something you need to be aware of yourself. As you are aware of this, you will be able to take steps to ensure your webinar is accomplishing this goal, and you will be able to get everything out of webinars you are supposed to be getting.

Of course, webinars are an advanced area of focus, as this is not something you are going to be doing right now—without any expert platform, and without your website set up as fully and completely as it should be (in case you haven't noticed, this book is something of a pyramid—where all the knowledge in the early portions of the book lay the foundation for the mountain of success we are building toward down the stretch!). So make sure you are first focusing on the elements explored early in the book…and then, work toward mastering these ideas being explored deeper in the book!

Here is an example of a successful webinar idea:

http://shop-on-shop.org/

Is this the New Lazy Man's Way to MAKE MONEY? Get Free Book here: https://dr-davies-school.thinkific.com/courses/

Continue To Expand Your Brand

<u>Realize: You ARE a brand!</u>

"I'm not a brand—I just run an Internet marketing website."

Wrong!

Regardless of what type of website you run—an affiliate site, an information product site, an Internet marketing site, doesn't matter—you need to think of yourself as a "brand." You need to see yourself as a "brand." You need to act accordingly. One of the greatest steps to success is realizing that you are a brand. Once you realize this, you will have an easier time convincing others that you are a brand as well…and this will make it much easier for you to benefit off of being a brand that people can follow, be loyal to, and stick with for years.

<u>Remain prominent in the public eye</u>

In addition to being a brand—as an individual, as a website, and as an entrepreneurial endeavor—you are going to want to make sure you are taking steps to remain prominent in the public eye. This means being extremely active on Twitter and other social media platforms. This means sticking with your video series and your webinars. This means keeping your newsletter active. This means always looking for opportunities to contribute off-site. The more prominent you are, the more you will remain in people's minds…and this will lead to continued traffic, continued engagement, continued conversions, and continued expansion!

Know the reputation you want to have

When people think of you, what do you want them to say? What do you want them to think? When people think of you—as a person, and as a brand—what reputation do you want to have?

As you may have noticed throughout the course of this book: most things we would like to happen do not happen by accident. The more intentional you are, the more likely you are to reach your goals!

Yes, once again, we are going to encourage you to take a break from this book for a moment. We know you're nearly to the finish line and you want to reach the end and say that you've done it, but before you read the next section, you need to take a bit of time. You need to define exactly what you want your reputation to be.

Continually cultivate this reputation

Once you have defined what you want your reputation to be, you will be able to take steps to continually cultivate this reputation. Again: these things don't happen by accident! So now that you've written down what you want your reputation to be, it's time for you to write down the things you feel you can do to cultivate this reputation.

What action steps can you take?

What can you do to continually grow and cultivate the reputation you want to have?

The more specific you are in your thoughts, goals, and ideas in this area, the more likely you will be to end up with the reputation you truly want to have. http://shop-on-shop.org/

Manage your reputation

And finally, you need to manage your reputation. This is different from cultivating your reputation; cultivating your reputation means, essentially, crafting and creating the reputation you want to have—painting the picture for the public that you want them to consume.

Managing your reputation, on the other hand, means paying attention to what *others* are saying about you online. Make sure there is not negative information—no negative thoughts or feedback—that is creating a negative picture of you for prospective customers. By actively paying attention to and managing your reputation, you will be able to cut off negative reputation elements at the root, and will be able to keep the good vibes flowing!

Continue To Expand Your Scope

Related products

In order to truly increase your business, one thing you need to do is expand your scope! If you can continually add new products and services, you will continually give existing customers new places to spend money, and you will continue to provide options that may appeal to prospective customers.

The first area where you should aim to expand your scope is through products of your own that relate to other products you already have out there. The more your products tie into one another, the more likely you are to discover that one sale is leading to lots of additional sales! Create great products…and then, create products the tie into or relate to the products you have already created.

Related areas of focus

Especially if you are in the "information marketing" game, another great way to expand your scope is by expanding your focus. You see, when you focus on only one area, you severely limit yourself and your ability to bring in profits. Of course, you do not want to try to focus on too many different areas at once, but if you are able to gradually add new areas of focus to the areas of focus you already, currently have, you will be able to continually increase your ceiling for profits.

New websites, products, etc.

And finally, you need to realize that there is no reason—absolutely no reason whatsoever—why you should only have one website, or one set of products. Your goal should ultimately be to build an empire online, and while this starts with one website and one set of ideas, you should continually be looking to expand it to new areas—to new websites, new products, and new ideas.

This is not something you need to be focusing on at the moment, as you should currently be focused on making your current project as great as it can be. But once you reach a point where you are in "expansion" realm instead of "improving" realm, it will be time for you to start looking toward the new websites and businesses you can create!

You can expand your brand, get similar products and get converting traffic for sales with the help of a free software package. To get the software giveaway go here:

http://www.getfreesoftwarefast.com

Continue To Focus

Know your goals

Finally, we want to encourage you and remind you to stay focused each day—and the first step of this is knowing your goals and reading through them each and every day (yes, each and every day!). As you do this, you will put yourself in position to continually chase and accomplish your goals. And, of course, our final admonishment to you:

Do what you can do each day!

How do you climb a mountain? One step at a time.

Do not allow yourself to get overwhelmed by the magnitude of what you are trying to accomplish. Instead, realize that there is only so much you can do each day…but as long as you are doing what you can do each day, you will continually move closer to your goals.

Tomorrow, wake up and ask yourself, "What can I do today to improve my future success?"

The next day, wake up and ask yourself the same question.

The next day, do the same. And the next day. And the next day. And the next.

Do what you can do each day. Truly, you will be amazed by just how much this enables you to accomplish!

It helps also joining and partnering with others who are already successful. See this sites for example:

http://www.webfire.com/a/?id=29029&aff=1

Is this the New Lazy Man's Way to MAKE MONEY? Get Free Book here: http://shop-on-shop.org/

To Learn More

Remember to claim your Free Bonus!

Free Traffic Training on How to Get Tons of Traffic to Your Website Without All the Complicated SEO:

http://www.webfire.com/a/?id=29029

In this Free Traffic Training, you will learn how to:

- Instantly get traffic in ANY niche
- Get free exposure from page one of Google, Yahoo, and Bing in 7 minutes or less
- Quickly and easily find people looking to buy what you could be selling
- How to target the traffic that brings in the money instead of fighting over the junk traffic that 99% of everyone else is going for.
- And lots, lots more!

About the Author:

Eur Ing Dr Davies M. Mulenga,

PhD MScEng BEng CEng MICE MVDI DBA THEOL

Formerly Structures Asset Manager on the £6,2 Billion Pounds Motorway Project in London UK, Dr Davies Mulenga is Managing Director of Huebl Group, a chartered Civil Structural Engineer, Pastor and bestseller co-author. Also, Principal Structures Consultant Dr Mulenga has worked as expert advisor on several high profile multi-million Pound projects in Europe and overseas. A game changer with over 25 years of remarkable experience in Engineering including Business and Asset Management.

He has also taught in Universities and stands as one of the most successful business and engineering talents of all time. Website: http://www.getfreesoftwarefast.com

Useful Website References:

http://www.globalonlineshop.co.uk/
http://www.getfreesoftwarefast.com
http://crowd1.com/signup/topmillionaire
http://www.webfire.com/a/?id=29029

https://dr-davies-school.thinkific.com/courses/
http://www.gigpanda.com
http://www.shop-for-shop.co.uk
http://www.getfreesoftwarefast.com/isf/optin.php
http://www.shop-on-shop.org/
http://www.shoppingsherlock.com/465048
http://invitation.shoppingsherlock.com/465048